Helper.
Rescuer.
Defender.

*Praying as the Wife God
Made You to Be.*

by Kim Gordon

Contributors: Alice Matthews Adopted by the Theology of Work Project Steering Committee February 4, 2017.

Theology of Work Project Online Materials by Theology of Work Project, Inc. is licensed under a Creative Commons Attribution-Noncommercial 4.0 International License based on a work at www.theologyofwork.org

Scripture quotations marked ESV are from the Holy Bible, English Standard Version, copyright © 2001 by Crossway Bibles, a publishing ministry of Good News Publishers. Used by permission. All rights reserved.

Scriptures marked NIV are taken from the NEW INTERNATIONAL VERSION (NIV): Scripture taken from THE HOLY BIBLE, NEW INTERNATIONAL VERSION ®. Copyright© 1973, 1978, 1984, 2011 by Biblica, Inc.™. Used by permission of Zondervan

Scripture quotations marked CSB have been taken from the Christian Standard Bible®, Copyright © 2017 by Holman Bible Publishers. Used by permission. Christian Standard Bible® and CSB® are federally registered trademarks of Holman Bible Publishers.

Scriptures marked NLT are taken from the HOLY BIBLE, NEW LIVING TRANSLATION (NLT): Scriptures taken from the HOLY BIBLE, NEW LIVING TRANSLATION, Copyright© 1996, 2004, 2007 by Tyndale House Foundation. Used by permission of Tyndale House Publishers, Inc., Carol Stream, Illinois 60188. All rights reserved. Used by permission

Scriptures marked NKJV are taken from the NEW KING JAMES VERSION (NKJV): Scripture taken from the NEW KING JAMES VERSION®. Copyright© 1982 by Thomas Nelson, Inc. Used by permission. All rights reserved.

Scriptures marked TLB are taken from the THE LIVING BIBLE (TLB): Scripture taken from THE LIVING BIBLE copyright© 1971. Used by permission of Tyndale House Publishers, Inc., Carol Stream, Illinois 60188. All rights reserved.

Scripture quotations marked MSG are taken from THE MESSAGE, copyright © 1993, 2002, 2018 by Eugene H. Peterson. Used by permission of NavPress. All rights reserved. Represented by Tyndale House Publishers, Inc.

Graphic design: *Steph Stewart Design*
Cover Photo: *Amanda Gall – A Fly on the Wall Photography*

Library of Congress Catalog Number:2023947757

Name:	Gordon, Kimberly Author
Title:	*Helper Rescuer Defender*
	Kim Gordon
	Advantage Books, 2023
Identifiers:	ISBN Paperback: 978159757481
	ISBN Hard Cover: 978159757597
	ISBN eBook: 978159757726
Subjects:	RELIGION: Christian Life – Inspirational
	RELIGION: Christian Life – Devotional
	RELIGION: Christian Life – Spiritual Growth

First Printing: Noverber 2023
23 24 25 26 27 28 10 9 8 7 6 5 4 3 2 1

This book is dedicated to my husband, Stewart. I've come to realize that God knew what he was doing when he drew us together. You have helped to raise me up from a time of complete brokenness to who I am supposed to be. Thank you for loving me big.

Contents

Contents

Contents

*Prayers for My Husband–
Tackling the Why*

*M*arriage isn't easy. I'll bet you already know that part; but stay with me! If you have a husband, he needs your help. Literally. In the time of creation God looked at man in the garden and said, (heavily paraphrasing here)… dude… you're very cool, but you need a helper. The culmination of creation only needed one thing to be complete, an adequate helper. That was the original purpose he created us for, ladies! To be a helper. So, what does being a helper really mean from God's perspective? How can we learn to be a helper in a way that is pleasing to Him? Does this mean to be merely an assistant? Does it convey our role as a subservient servant to our respective husbands? Let's look for the answer in the original Hebrew words used in scripture.

The Hebrew word for helper is ezer. It was used twice in Genesis to describe the woman as God created her in

Eden. In most other instances where this word appears in the scriptures, it was used to describe Yahweh, the original name for the one and only God of Israel. The word that describes who we are to be to our husbands is the same word used to describe our loving and awesome God himself! Ezer depicts the image of a rescuer (helper) and defender (shield); of an ally who comes running heroically to a cry for help. In contrast, the Hebrew word for servant is eved which brings the connotation of a task-doer who is owned and subordinate. Our God would never be reduced to just a subordinate task-doer. According to theologyofwork.org, the use of the word ezer to describe women overturns the idea of simple subordinance to men, and instead offers the overture that "woman was not created to serve the man, but to serve with the man". God's observation that man's condition of aloneness was "not good" indicates that He created woman to be man's partner in stewarding all that God had provided…and to provide a suitable helper as a solution. Let this rest on your spirit for a moment, ladies. You are not an afterthought meant only to get the socks washed and the dusting done. The word that God chooses to describe you in relationship to your husband is ezer…the same powerful word that describes God's help for us! God's help that rescues and saves humanity. God's help that is full of love and mercy and grace. God's help that is surprising and steadfast and faithful. God's help that anticipates our needs and provides abundantly. The fact that the Eden woman was described in scripture as ezer, a person with helping capabilities of this magnitude, is nothing short of mind-blowing! The God of heaven has graciously gifted us as women with the qualities it takes to be a true helper, a rescuer and defender, to our husband… qualities that reflect God's own character in the way that He is a helper to us.

Now let's go a little deeper: you are the only one assigned to this role. God supernaturally delegated you as your husband's helper. You are chosen to intervene and intercede in helping your husband become all that he was meant to be. It is only when we relinquish our own control and choose to partner with God through prayer that our help can be effective.

Does this understanding change the way you see your role in your marriage? Does it alter your connotation of your job as a 'helper'? Does it breathe fresh life into how you see yourself? Gone are the days of thinking that you are nothing more than an underpaid refrigerator organizer. You no longer must create your own role as a wife, or pattern it after the marriage of your parents or other role models. God established a clear role for you as a wife; an important one. A role that values you, and one that works.

Prayer changes things. With your prayers on his behalf, your husband can become more and accomplish more than ever possible without you. You can help him reach his calling; in fact, you are imperative to him for that reason. Lifting someone to the feet of Jesus is the most powerful way that we can be a helper. As we do this, God provides revelation and insight. He magnifies our capability to sense needs and to partner with Him in provision. He grants us peace. He is pleased and responds with His sovereign help. This shift within my own mindset liberated me to realize that God created me to be a helper of this magnitude. This is why he created me with an intuitive nature so that I can often perceive what is going on with my husband and what his needs may be. The same is true for you. And when I am unsure, or when he is resistant, my omnipotent, omniscient, and omnipresent God certainly knows what he needs. I am unafraid to go over my husband's head to the only one who loves him more than I do!

Learning to lift my husband to the throne has changed my husband, changed our marriage, and changed me. It has distinctively given my personal relationship with God a new depth. Whether you're newly married, new to faith, or have come up against a new challenge, I hope that a glimpse of the way that I've learned to talk with our loving and kind heavenly father will be a catalyst for your change, too, so that you can experience the benefits of that change in your marriage and in your own personal walk with the one true and living God.

I encourage you to pray together with your husband whenever you can. Praying together invites God into your relationship in a powerful way. Praying together helps us to still our souls, and then gain some perspective on what is happening in our lives. It opens the door for Jesus to come into our relationship in a dynamic way and invites him to cast light on every aspect of our relationship. More specifically, it allows us to see our circumstances and the condition of our hearts from an eternal perspective, not just from the narrow perspective of the here and now. We can then walk forward with renewed faith and vision that is based on God's perspective and not our own.

The passages you'll find in these daily prayers are vulnerable and personal; you will need to tweak them for your husband's character, personality, personal struggles, and where he is in his own faith-walk. Mark them up and make them your own; make them specific. I'm hopeful that this writing of my prayers will be helpful to you in developing confidence for your own personal conversations with God, and in strengthening your man and your marriage. I pray that it will encourage you to be an even more influential helper to your husband, adding dimension to your convictions and your personal walk with Jesus. May you experience the blessing of realizing that prayer moves mountains and breathes life into the situations of our lives. And as you pass this little prayer book from friend to friend, maybe we can collectively be a part of a huge rising up of godly women who are influencing this world with the light and life of Jesus. Can you imagine how the world would be different? Families, children, even generations can be changed by our learning to lean into Jesus on behalf of husbands and fathers. My hope is that this little book will serve to reflect God's model for how to be the ezer for your husband and will start a movement that radically changes how we as women pursue our role as a wife in a way that pleases the God of eternity. My personal email is in the back of the book; I would love for you to send me a note and let me know what happens as you habitually spend time with God on behalf of your marriage and your husband.

Preparing Your Heart and Mindset for Prayer

*I*t is helpful to have a daily morning prayer time in a place that is quiet and serene. Once I can approach the throne fully and without distraction, I can often carry that place of serenity and connection in my heart the rest of the day no matter where I go.

Writing prayers out is a practice that makes my prayers more meaningful and ingrains them in my heart. It helps to resume where I left off when I take a few minutes to pray among the distractions of daily life. I believe that it also helps to develop a higher awareness of the evidence of God's answers. We've included writing space with each prayer page so that you can begin the practice of writing your own prayers out.

There are impressions that the Holy Spirit has placed on my heart over time; realizations that I've experienced through spending time in Bible study and prayer that have motivated me to develop a pattern and pray regardless of circumstances. Using these as guidelines helps to prepare my mindset and enter the presence of my Lord.

Pray first for your husband's wife! Ask God to purify your heart and thoughts, to help you set aside any selfish intentions, and to focus on God's best for your husband and marriage. *(Matthew 5:8; Proverbs 16:2, Philippians 2:3)*

Pray for your husband and marriage out of love for God and commitment to your marriage, no matter how you feel in any given moment, and despite what you think he deserves. *(Jeremiah 33:3; Romans 12:9–12)*

Pray for your husband with faith in God's mercy and grace and power. *(James 1:6; James 5:13–16)*

Pray for your husband with authority; the power of the resurrected Christ lives in you! Your prayers are a powerful agent of change. *(Romans 8:11)*

Pray for your husband as if you are one; you are. When you lift your husband in prayer you are also praying for yourself; you are one flesh in his eyes. *(Mark 10:8)*

Pray for your husband steadfastly and continually. *(1 Thessalonians 5:17-21)*

Know that God adores you as a daughter. Your prayers for your husband are within the circle of God's will for your life and for the fulfillment of your role as a wife. You are specifically given authority to pray over your husband in a way that no one else can. Your Heavenly Father is pleased with and pays careful attention to your prayers, and He responds with divine intervention. *(1 John 5:14-15)*

Then the Lord God said, "It is not good that the man should be alone; I will make him a helper fit for him. (Genesis 2:18 ESV)

She brings him good, not harm, all the days of her life. (Proverbs 31:12 NIV)

If you abide in me, and my words abide in you, ask whatever you wish, and it will be done for you. (John 15:7 ESV)

This is the confidence we have before him: If we ask anything according to his will, he hears us. And if we know that he hears whatever we ask, we know that we have what we have asked of him. (1 John 5:14-15 CSB)

1.

A Prayer of Gratitude for My Husband

eavenly Father, I am grateful for my husband and lift him up to you today. I don't always remember to tell him or you how much I love him and am grateful for his presence in my life. He is a gift. Thank you for making him in your image. I praise you for the man that he is, and for who you created him to be. Thank you for claiming him as a son; thank you for giving his life purpose. I realize that we are all on a journey to become the person you created us to be, and I pray that I will be the wife who lifts him up to connect with you in every way. I want to help him reach his calling. I am grateful that he seeks to protect and provide for our family and works tirelessly to do so. I praise you for his physical strength and his headstrong nature and his amazing intelligence. I praise you for his funny nature and the things he comes up with to make people laugh. I praise you for the things he teaches me. I praise you for his determination and drive. I praise you for his curiosity about you and about eternal life. I praise you for his leadership, for his desire to teach and train people, and in that way to raise up leaders and give of himself to others. Most of all, God, I so adore his strength and power in provision and protection but also his distinct ability to care for me and our family gently and gracefully. I thank you for giving him a heart to love me. Thank you for leading his heart to mine, and for aligning everything so that we could spend the rest of our lives together. Father, I ask you for wisdom and a pure heart, so that I can intercede on his behalf in his best interest and according to your will. Let your respect and honor for me be my guide for showing respect and honor to my husband. Help me to be the helper, rescuer, and defender he needs to accomplish all that you have for him in his life.

Every time I think of you, I give thanks to my God. (Philippians 1:3 NLT)

Give thanks in all circumstances; for this is the will of God in Christ Jesus for you. (1 Thessalonians 5:18 ESV)

Give thanks to the Lord, for he is good, for his steadfast love endures forever. (Psalm 136:1 ESV)

Reflection:

Have I disciplined myself to live in gratitude for my husband and for the dimension he adds to my life? Might I be less inclined to take my husband for granted when I spend time thanking God for him and for all the good that he adds to my life?

Notes

_____

_____

_____

_____

_____

_____

_____

_____

_____

_____

_____

_____

_____

_____

_____

_____

_____

_____

_____

2.

Physical, Emotional, and Spiritual Health

*H*eavenly Father, I lift my husband, _____, before your feet at the throne today. I thank you that you are his protection and that his safety comes from you. I thank you for the healing that you have already blessed him with. I ask that you station angels around our home and the places where he stays when he is away; angels who will guide him away from danger and protect him from harm. Thank you for being his refuge of safety, security, and protection. I ask that you cleanse and strengthen every system and organ of his physical body; bless him with long life, exuberant health, and invigorated strength. Increase the desire in both of us to be physically fit and to grow in stamina. Grant us motivation for healthy nutritional choices. Give nutrition to his body and soul. Grant him restful sleep, Father, and be his security. Bless him with mobility and agility to perform tasks but also to enjoy life. Let no harm come to him. Spare him from illness, disease, addiction. I ask that you place within him a calm spirit that helps him to manage overwhelm and stress from the requirements and schedule of his work environment. Plant within him a deep desire for relationship with you. Guard his heart, Father. Create the knowledge in him to keep his Bible close and to go to your word for answers. Place within his heart a deep curiosity that seeks your heart first and constantly; a desire that is conducive to learning who you are in every circumstance and to recognizing your ways. Prompt him to share with you all his burdens and fears. Give him the heart to look to Jesus as a constant guide for his choices and to model the life and love of Christ in every relationship. Father, your word tells us in John 15 to live in you, to stay connected to you as a branch to a vine; that separated from you, we are deadwood. Place in my husband a desire to stay connected to you through your word, knowing that this relationship leads to refined thoughts and behaviors, to clarified purpose, to distilled choices, to purification of our hearts.

The Lord is my strength and my shield; my heart trusts in him, and he helps me. My heart leaps for joy, and with my song I praise him. (Psalm 28:7 NIV)

Dear friend, I pray that you may enjoy good health and that all may go well with you, even as your soul is getting along well. (3 John 1:2 NIV)

I can do all things through Christ who strengthens me. (Philippians 4:13 NKJV)

*Bless the Lord, O my soul, and forget not all his
benefits, who forgives all your iniquity, who heals
all your diseases, who redeems your life from the
pit, who crowns you with steadfast love and mercy.
(Psalm103:2-4 ESV)*

Reflection:

*Am I developing the knowledge and skills to help my
husband to be healthy, strong, vibrant, and at ease? Am
I inspiring my husband to seek the face of God and the
kingdom of Heaven? Am I giving him space to spend time
with Jesus?*

Notes

_____

_____

_____

_____

_____

_____

_____

_____

_____

_____

_____

_____

_____

_____

_____

3.

Courage

*H*eavenly Father, I know that my husband steps into a world of chaos every day that tries his faith and tests his resolve; a world where deception whirls around him. I know that you love him as a son and want him to stay within your will with his actions and reactions. I praise you for providing certainty and unshakable confidence as the foundation of our faith in passages like Psalm 27:3. I pray that you teach my husband to walk daily with you, to come to know your character and your promises, and to look to you first for answers. Establish his belief in your word and discernment for your leading so that he will know when he is walking in obedience. I ask you to give him the courage to always stand boldly in the love of Christ, and to make bold decisions that are underscored by grace. Increase the depth of his faith and wisdom, Lord. Help him to stay in the center of your will and to make right decisions without wavering. Infuse him with the courage to turn his back on sin. Give him grace and discernment to make decisions using the mindset of Christ, modeling His love and compassion for all people. Help him to be aware of unique differences among people, and to realize that those differences are attributable to your creation. Let him be known as a man of integrity. Build within him a confidence stemming from his relationship with you that allows him to courageously face his adversaries, knowing when to roar as the Lion, and when to be silent or walk away as Jesus sometimes did. Ephesians 6 shows us that although Paul lived in a fragmented world, that he remained unified by focusing on Your word and prayer as the essentials of life. Though my husband also lives in a fragmented world, Father, help him to unclutter his life and mind by focusing daily on scripture and prayer. I pray that my husband, like Paul, will constantly refuse to be pulled away from his relationship with Christ.

Be strong and courageous. Do not be afraid or terrified because of them, for the LORD your God goes with you; he will never leave you nor forsake you. (Deuteronomy 31:6 NIV)

For God gave us a spirit not of fear but of power and love and self-control. (2 Timothy 1:7 ESV)

This is my command — be strong and courageous! Do not be afraid or discouraged. For the Lord your God is with you wherever you go. (Joshua 1:9 NLT)

Reflection:

Am I providing a calm and restful environment in our home? Do I remember to show my husband appreciation for and understanding about his work? Am I an encourager to him? Do I build him up by listening well?

Notes

_____

_____

_____

_____

_____

_____

_____

_____

_____

_____

_____

_____

_____

_____

_____

_____

_____

_____

_____

_____

4.

Leadership and Wisdom

 $\mathscr{F}$ ather, I thank you for giving my husband the gift of administration. I praise you for calling him to be a leader. In Jeremiah 3, you set the standard for leaders to be shepherds after your own heart. Draw my husband near to you and help him to vigilantly seek your heart so that he can lead by Christs' example. So very much is required of my husband daily, dear Lord, and yet one of the biggest callings you've assigned to him is leadership in our home and community. Help him to realize this. I know he becomes work worn and weary with constant decision making and leadership of his family and others. Reinforce him with grace and humility to submit to you as Lord, then in turn with the courage to spiritually lead our home. Create in him a desire to see and support spiritual growth in me and in others. Give him spiritual eyes that see other people according to their potential and not their performance. As he fulfills his roles, lay on his spirit motivation from Christ's life and leadership to inspire him that his sacrifice is worthwhile. Refresh his spirit daily with biblical knowledge to encourage him that leadership should be marked by your influence, not by dictatorship, and always wrapped up in love and respect for others. Give him discernment to sift through monumental tasks and communication each day and to prioritize what to attend to himself and what to delegate to others. Help him to manage his marriage, family, and work by keeping in mind that the head of every man is Christ (1 Corinthians 11:3), and to exemplify the attributes of Christ in action and in voice. Give him wisdom and discernment for making both big and small decisions. Help him to always remember to look to you for that wisdom and discernment in the choices and decisions he must make. Give him the peace of knowing that he is never alone, but that the Creator of the universe goes before him and will be with him always (Deuteronomy 31:8).

If you need wisdom, ask our generous God, and he will give it to you. He will not rebuke you for asking. (James 1:5 NLT)

My prayer for you is that you will overflow more and more with love for others, and at the same time keep on growing in spiritual knowledge and insight, for I want you always to see clearly the difference between right and wrong, and to be inwardly clean, no one being able to criticize you from now until our Lord returns. (Philippians 1:9-10 TLB)

For even the Son of Man did not come expecting to be served but to serve and give his life in exchange for the salvation of many. (Matthew 20:28 TPT)

Reflection:

Am I setting a good example in our household for seeing others in a positive light? Do I remind my husband of the good influence that he is in other people's lives? Does my husband know that I view him as a leader?

Notes

_____

_____

_____

_____

_____

_____

_____

_____

_____

_____

_____

_____

_____

_____

_____

_____

_____

5.

Healing and Freedom

*F*ather, you have promised peace that stands guard over our hearts and minds (Philippians 4:7). I thank you and give you praise for this gracious gift. I pray that you give my husband an inner peace about the freedom that you have provided for his life through Christs' work on the cross and through salvation. Grant him serenity and healing from the pain of his past and the scars that Satan has left on his heart. Help him to recognize that through his relationship with you that he is truly free from that brokenness. But help him remember how the brokenness feels so that he can help and be compassionate toward others who are hurting. Draw close to him so he will draw closer to you. Help him to learn to cast every burden and anxiety at your feet and release them to your love for him. Heal any feelings of insignificance, inferiority, or self-doubt with complete restoration based on biblical truth. I ask you to show him that his self-worth is not based on his work or his status in this world, but on what you think of him; help him see himself through your eyes. Whenever he doubts his self-worth, help him to remember the cross and how much you love him. Free him from the constraint and oppression of lies that he has been told in the past; I ask that you make him aware of these wounds, and of the judgments that result. Touch his heart and mind and heal him of those wounds so that he can live the life of freedom that you intend for him. I praise you that you are his Father, his Healer, and his Redeemer.

So much social and cultural pressure is placed on men in this world, Father God, give him freedom from any undue pressures that he places on himself. Give him the ability to discern what is important to you, his Savior, for his life. Place deep within him the knowledge that the fruit of being a husband is in providing space for a strong, confident, spiritually mature wife and family. Give him courage to allow that growth and restoration to take place. Bring his spirit under the authority of Jesus and break any generational chains that bind him or create fear.

Trust in the Lord with all your heart, and do not lean on your own understanding. In all your ways acknowledge him, and he will make straight your paths. (Proverbs 3:5-6 ESV)

The mind governed by the flesh is death, but the mind governed by the Spirit is life and peace. (Romans 8:6 NIV)

Cast all your anxiety on him because he cares for you. (1 Peter 5:7 NIV)

Reflection:

Does my husband get the opportunity to glimpse the way that I see him rather than dwelling on untruths about himself that he has been told in the past? Am I an encourager to his spiritual growth and maturity? Do I remind him of how deeply loved he is… by me and by God?

Notes

_____

_____

_____

_____

_____

_____

_____

_____

_____

_____

_____

_____

_____

6.

Success within Your Will

*F*ather, I know that the dreams you have placed in my husband's heart were placed there intentionally. I ask that you make me sensitive to his dreams; help me to see them clearly so that I can be his biggest encourager. I pray for _____ now that he realizes those dreams in real life, that he comes to know that you long to celebrate with him as he achieves success, as do I. Help him to see success through an eternal lens, Lord, and not only from the viewpoint of this world. When he is between opportunities, Father, or when he is uncertain of next steps, remind him that your word provides a lamp for his feet and a light to his path (Psalm 119:105), and that you will illuminate his way as he stays focused on you and seeks your will.

I praise you for the experiences and successes that my husband has had in the marketplace, and for the skills that he has developed. Bless his efforts in his work, Lord. I admire how _____ strives for excellence and to do his best; bless the efforts of his hands and his mind to create productivity for himself, his team, and his business. I appreciate that his efforts bless and positively affect those around him. His work ethic is inspiring, father, and I ask that he be rewarded appropriately for his efforts as you are glorified through his efforts and successes. Remove or alter obstacles that would keep him from success. I pray that you open doors of opportunity for him and walk him right on through them, especially if you created him to do something other than what he is currently doing. Posture him to see those opportunities, and to know that you divinely coordinate the people that cross his path as well as his gifts, talents, and the passions that bring him enjoyment.

I pray that you bless my husband financially with more than enough. Prosper him through your grace and favor. I have never seen anyone as giving as he is, and I know that is a quality that you put within his heart. Allow him to know the joy of extraordinary giving as you provide lavishly for him. Allow him to be in a position where he can point toward you as his light, and people know that there is no way he could have achieved to that place without the blessing and grace of our God. Bless our marriage and our home with abundance so that we can give abundantly. And in all things, in all things, Lord, help him to glorify you.

Commit to the LORD whatever you do, and he will establish your plans. (Proverbs 16:3 NIV)

"And you shall remember the Lord your God, for it is He who gives you power to get wealth, that He may establish His covenant which He swore to your fathers, as it is this day."
(Deuteronomy 8:18 NKJV)

Whatever you do, work at it with all your heart, as working for the Lord, not for human masters, since you know that you will receive an inheritance from the Lord as a reward. It is the Lord Christ you are serving. (Colossians 3:23-24 NIV)

Reflection:

Do I give space for and speak of my husband's dreams? Does he know that I see him as successful? Does he know that I believe in him? Does he know that I pray for him, his work, his opportunities?

Notes

_____

_____

_____

_____

_____

_____

_____

_____

_____

_____

_____

7.

Creativity, Relaxation, and Rest

*H*eavenly Father, thank you for giving my husband an interest in a fun hobby that he enjoys. I love the way it soothes his soul and gives him joy. Thank you for his creativity and attention to detail. It is inspirational that you, our Creator, are the inspiration for the creativity within us. Bless my husband with efficiency at work and therefore the extra time to pursue his hobbies and interests that you have placed in his soul. Help him realize that he can glorify you through taking time for pleasure and rest. Help me to be a fun and supportive partner in the things that give him joy! Give me the inspiration to create a space and time where he can easily participate in and truly enjoy the things that give him joy. Remind me to take the time to hang out with him sometimes while he is engaged in the things that interest him, as it provides a perfect opportunity for easy conversation, laughter,

and to show interest in him. I ask you to combine
_____'s interests, hobbies, gifts, talents, and
experiences into the perfectly paved road for what
you created him to do.

Heavenly father, you have so abundantly blessed us
with our home. Thank you for providing us with
shelter, safety, comforts. I pray that it is a place of
peace and a place where the Holy Spirit abides in us
and with us. Help me to care for our home in such a
way that it provides peace and serenity for my husband so that he can be at rest when he is home. Give
me the grace and energy to care for our home well,
to create an atmosphere of comfort and love for our
family and friends. May anyone who comes into our
home be blessed by an atmosphere of warmth and
hospitality and love. I pray that the way I care for our
home is seen by my husband as an act of service and
love, and that this will always be a place where we
can come into your presence to grow, to heal, to rest,
to dream, and to recover.

> *Come to me, all you who labor and are heavy laden,*
> *and I will give you rest. Take my yoke upon you and*
> *learn from Me, for I am gentle and lowly in heart,*
> *and you will find rest for your souls. For My yoke is*
> *easy, and My burden is light.*
> *(Matthew 11:28–30 NKJV)*
>
> *By wisdom a house is built, and by understanding it*
> *is established; by knowledge the rooms are filled with*
> *all precious and pleasant riches.*
> *(Proverbs 24:3–4 ESV)*

My people will abide in a peaceful habitation, in secure dwellings, and in quiet resting places. (Isaiah 32:18 ESV)

Reflection:

Does my husband know that I support his dreams and hobbies? Do I encourage him to take time away from work to restore his soul through activities that he loves to do? Do I care for our home in a way that encourages my family to enjoy life and to take time for rest and respite?

Notes

_____

_____

_____

_____

_____

_____

_____

_____

_____

_____

_____

_____

_____

_____

_____

_____

_____

8.

Protection and Provision

*D*ear Lord, as I pray over my husband tonight, he is away from home working. I release all my worries and anxiety to you as he travels, knowing that his protection is found in you. Thank you for the work you have given him, and for the favor that he has in his career. I pray that you would continue to bless him in his work. Sometimes the hours and days that he needs to be away from home are difficult, Lord, for both of us. I pray that you dispatch a legion of angels to assemble around him and provide safety, strength and soundness of mind, spirit, and body. Place a hedge of protection around him from negativity and darkness, and from anyone who would harm him. Comfort the unrest in his heart caused from being away from home and from me. I know that you love _____ and call him Son, and I ask for your loving, comprehensive protection to surround him. Help me be creative with ways to communicate with him and be supportive when we are separate. Influence my words to smash any insecurities that may arise. Let us not be swept away with runaway thoughts that become negative and lead to frustration or fear. Sway our spirits to lean into you, as 2 Corinthians 10:5 teaches, tearing down barriers that are constructed against your truth, and taking every thought captive to make it obedient to Christ.

Thank you for all the ways you have equipped _____ for the work that he does and the way he provides for our family. I praise you for the talents, skills, insight, and perseverance you have instilled in him that allow him to perform with excellence in his work. Thank you that as he labors on earth for your glory and your kingdom, that he is also laying up treasures in heaven for another day. Guide my husband in the knowledge that, together, we can live life graciously and abundantly within the circle of your love and will. Help him to maintain an eternal perspective about his work and not become obsessed with it in any way. Help us both to realize that his opportunities are gifts from you, and not solely based on himself. Continue to renew his mindset to realize that his work is a vehicle to glorify you. Protect and provide for him as he constantly strives to protect and provide for me and to live for you. Train him to lean into you as the antithesis of his fears. Remind him that you are for him, regardless of who comes against him. Help him to be guided by his love for you rather than by fears. Place in his spirit the truth and knowledge that you are our provision and will care for us, just like the lilies and the sparrows, no matter what circumstances present themselves around us. Guard his heart, I pray, and keep him grounded within the circle of your love. Give me the grace to remind him to cast all his concerns and anxieties on you as his redeemer. Help him to always recognize your love, protection, and provision for him.

The Lord keeps you from all harm and watches over your life. The Lord keeps watch over you as you come and go, both now and forever.
(Psalm 121:7-8 NLT)

The Lord is with me; I will not be afraid. What can mere mortals do to me? (Psalm 118:6 NIV)

But the Lord is faithful, and he will strengthen you and protect you from the evil one.
(2 Thessalonians 3:3 NIV)

May the favor of the Lord our God rest on us; establish the work of our hands for us — yes, establish the work of our hands. (Psalm 90:17 NIV)

Reflection:

Am I grounded in my own faith so that I can strengthen and undergird my husband in difficult times? Am I a calming influence on my husband? Do I help him establish total trust in our God as I model fully trusting him for our life and provision?

Notes

_____

_____

_____

_____

_____

_____

_____

_____

_____

_____

_____

_____

_____

_____

_____

_____

_____

_____

_____

9.

Teamwork within Our Marriage

*F*ather, I thank you for our marriage. I pray for my husband to see that developing and growing a strong marriage and family is one of his primary responsibilities. I pray for our marriage and family unit to honor you, God, and that we honor you with our lives. Help him to use the example and inspiration of Christ to place the needs of his wife above his own, bringing glory to you in the process. Place in my heart the desire to place my husband's needs above my own to bring that glory full circle within our family. Soften our hearts to fall in love a little bit more every day, and to prioritize our marriage without fail. Allow us to complement each other so obviously that his strengths fill in the blanks for what I don't do well, and that his weaknesses simply become my place to shine. Help me to be his ezer, his helper, as you intended. I desire to see him live out his destiny. I ask that you reveal to me ways that I can truly support him in the desires that you have placed in his heart. Nudge my spirit to anticipate his needs and desires, and to tend to feelings of emptiness that he may not even recognize. Grant us vision to see past words and wounds, beyond who we are being to who we can be under your grace. Your word teaches us that all things are possible for someone who believes (Mark 9:23); Lord, help any unbelief that we have. Through our belief we can be certain that every aspect of our lives and marriage will be transformed. Father, you know our temperaments, our weaknesses, our frustrations, and the areas where we have conflict. Show us ways to love each other fully, and to develop patience with each other's idiosyncrasies. Give us the grace to talk through making major decisions with the least amount of misunderstanding and conflict. Provide opportunities for us to grow as individuals and together as a couple; prompt us to recognize those chances, and to take advantage of them. Help us to respect each other even in difficult times. Over and over, God, remind us that as we grow closer to you, we grow closer to each other. And above all things, Lord, flood our hearts with the desire to submit our marriage to the authority of Jesus every single day.

And the LORD God said, "It is not good that man should be alone; I will make him a helper comparable to him." Out of the ground the LORD God formed every beast of the field and every bird of the air, and brought them to Adam to see what he would call them. And whatever Adam called each living creature, that was its name. So Adam gave names to all cattle, to the birds of the air, and to every beast of the field. But for Adam there was not found a helper comparable to him. And the LORD God caused a deep sleep to fall on Adam, and he slept; and He took one of his ribs, and closed up the flesh in its place. Then the rib which the LORD God had taken from man He made into a woman, and He brought her to the man. And Adam said:

> *"This is now bone of my bones*
> *And flesh of my flesh;*
> *She shall be called Woman,*
> *Because she was taken out of Man."*

Therefore a man shall leave his father and mother and be joined to his wife, and they shall become one flesh. And they were both naked, the man and his wife, and were not ashamed.
(Genesis 2:18-25 NKJV)

Reflection:

Do I bring God honor in how I handle my marriage, and in the way that I love my husband? Do I keep in mind that love is an action, and not just a "feeling" to receive? Do I love my husband in the way that Christ loves me? Do I show respect to my husband in a way that he can receive it?

Notes

_____

_____

_____

_____

_____

_____

_____

_____

_____

_____

_____

_____

_____

_____

_____

_____

_____

_____

10.

Temptation Thrown in His Path

*H*eavenly Father, I thank you for the loyal heart that you have given my husband. Still, 1 Peter 5:8 warns us that our enemy prowls around like a roaring lion looking for someone to devour. I lift prayers for _____ and ask you to help him know that the enemy's attacks are very real; to be watchful and resist temptation. Strengthen him to choose to abstain from anything that would lead him to physical attraction outside our marriage or to any other entity that would tear us apart. Give him eyes and affection only for you, and for me. Our minds and hearts are under constant battle in this world, Father, especially for temporary satisfaction. I pray that you would give him a keen sense of awareness when he is being influenced by the deceiver. Strengthen him to always replace tempting thoughts with biblical truth and with devotion to you. Keep our marriage pure with Christ at the core. You love and know _____ so much better than I do, Father. You know the longings of his heart, his restlessness, and the searching of his soul. Please fill him with goodness and with good things. Influence him to always see the good that you have placed around him. Draw him into closer relationship with you, Father. Teach him to infuse his mind and soul with messages and music that sets his mind on you. I pray that more and more he will listen to and watch things that align with kingdom principles. Place within his very soul the desire to seek satisfaction only in you. Make him aware of his feelings, but not ruled by them. Your word tells us that sometimes the heart of a man is prone to stubbornness, deception, and pride (Mark 7: 20-22). Saturate my husband's heart with your truths and humility. Train him to use every resource you've given him to resist temptation and the evil one. Keep his faith focused on you, and not on any so-called human wisdom. Thank you for equipping my husband with the weapons and the strength of his Savior to stifle anything the enemy throws his way.

Do not conform to the pattern of this world, but be transformed by the renewing of your mind. Then you will be able to test and approve what God's will is—his good, pleasing and perfect will.
(Romans 12:2 NIV)

Above all else, guard your heart, for everything you do flows from it.(Proverbs 4:23 NIV)

Keep vigilant watch over your heart; that's where life starts. Don't talk out of both sides of your mouth; avoid careless banter, white lies, and gossip. Keep your eyes straight ahead; ignore all sideshow distractions. Watch your step, and the road will stretch out smooth before you. Look neither right nor left; leave evil in the dust.(Proverbs 4:23-27 MSG)

Reflection:

Am I watchful and observant of my husband and his times of restlessness to the best of my ability? Do I encourage him to look to your truths and promises as the foundation for his life?

Notes

_____

_____

_____

_____

_____

_____

_____

_____

_____

_____

_____

_____

_____

_____

11.

Connection and Communication
within Our Marriage

$\mathcal{H}$eavenly Father, some days are so hard. Sometimes we just don't understand each other – responses, reactivity, words, expressions – and sometimes we just read in too much of our own stuff. Attitudes stink. Triggers are snatched. Negative emotions can flare up in a heartbeat. Help us both to realize that we have natural differences, physiologically and emotionally, and that our backgrounds and experiences influence how we respond to circumstances. Just train us to take that first couple of seconds to tamp down that rising negative reaction and give a little grace. Remind us to filter our words with love, despite our feelings. Let kindness encompass our responses to each other. Break the strongholds of legalism that we may not even be aware of, and replace them with the mind of Christ. Place within us both the desire to complement each other through healthy communication and companionship. Let love, respect, and support help us gravitate toward each other at every turn. Mature and develop our hearts to pray for each other, even more in the rough times. Remind us to apply Romans 12 to our lives, that as we fix our attention on you, God, that we'll be changed from the inside out. Give me grace to see what's not working and to be willing to try a different way; and help me to keep the lines of communication open. Give me the capability to manage his powerful nature with dignity, grace, and gentleness. Give us both grace to be able to see what kind of communication doesn't work between us and an openness to new ways of communicating that do work. Help him to see me as you do, as a daughter of the King. Help me to see him as you do, as a son and direct descendant of the almighty God. Transform our hearts every day to love each other better than yesterday. Let his strengths (that sometimes drive me crazy!) become my pillars of support and let any weaknesses that I perceive in him become my place to show your glory a little more. Bless the union of our marriage, Lord, and bring our connection and communication constantly under the authority of Jesus Christ. Thank you, Jesus, for providing a way for us when we can't see a way through a tough time or situation.

Guard your words and you'll guard your life, but if your don't control your tongue, it will ruin everything. (Proverbs 13:3 TPT)

Husbands, love your wives, and do not be harsh with them. (Colossians 3:19 ESV)

Wives, in the same way submit yourselves to your own husbands so that, if any of them do not believe the word, they may be won over without words by the behavior of their wives, when they see the purity and reverence of your lives. (1 Peter 3: 1-2 NIV)

Reflection:
Do I keep banging my head against the same wall, or do I look for new ways to communicate that actually work with both of our personalities? Am I hanging onto pride or selfishness in not wanting to change anything about how I want us to connect? Am I looking to you, God, and allowing you to transform my mind and heart?

Notes

_____

_____

_____

_____

_____

_____

_____

_____

_____

_____

_____

_____

_____

_____

12.

Connection and Communication with Others

𝓕ather God, thank you for the personal growth that you have afforded my husband with regard to communicating effectively with others. Thank you for his mindset of excellence, and that he is a good leader and friend to others. Give _____ the grace to respect all others that he crosses paths with at work or in life, to see them as your creation, and to respond always with the power of your love. Remind him that leaders set standards, and not just goals. I pray that you flood his soul with awareness of what his Creator has done for him. I pray that you give him the discernment to remain focused on you for literal renewing and transformation of his mind. I ask that you give him the wisdom to reframe every situation, conversation, and response with the light of Christ. I pray that his greatest demonstration for others is how his God brings out the best in him and fully develops his life as a result of his focus on you.

I ask that you grant my husband discernment, Lord, in relationships. Help him to walk away when he needs to, as Jesus did at times, and to focus on those who are reliable and who will walk with him on the path ahead. Create a desire in his heart for constant communication with you, Lord, and bless him with prompting from the Holy Spirit to pray and to listen to your leading. Remind him daily that his walk with Christ affects all other relationships, and that he can't be his best as a friend, employee, boss, or husband without Christ as his partner. Impress on his heart to look on others with the love of Christ, not with judgment. Remind him to be quick to hear, slow to speak, slow to anger. Help him to realize that we are to do everything to the glory of God, even when it comes to our connection and communication with others.

> *Know this, my beloved brothers: let every person be quick to hear, slow to speak, slow to anger. (James 1:19 ESV)*
>
> *But you are a chosen race, a royal priesthood, a holy nation, a people for his own possession, that you may proclaim the excellencies of him who called you out of the darkness into his marvelous light. (1 Peter 2:9 ESV)*
>
> *Above all, constantly echo God's intense love for one another, for love will be a canopy over a multitude of sins. (1 Peter 4:8 TPT)*

Reflection:

Do I model graciousness for my husband in how I treat others? Do I show my husband grace? Do I treat him and others with respect?

Notes

13.

Awareness of His Influence

*T*hank you for giving my husband an amicable nature and the ability to tell mesmerizing stories, and for the desire in his heart to always be sharing and teaching. Plant within him an awareness of the influence that his teachings and storytelling have upon me and others. Give him the realization that you have brought him to a place where someone is always watching him, and that he is responsible for passing the character of Christ on to others. Encourage him to see how he has impacted others in the past, and his potential to impact others today. Condition him to be aware that how he manages his life, time, choices, and relationships is a daily example to those you have placed around him. Help him to realize that his words either build up or tear down, and to choose them carefully. Father, your word tells us in Galatians 5: 22-23 about the fruits produced by the Holy Spirit in our lives. I love the way these qualities are presented in The Passion Translation that so beautifully help me understand the attributes that indicate a relationship with Jesus. I pray for continual development of each of these in my husband's life today; for love in all its varied expressions, joy that overflows, peace that subdues, patience that endures, kindness in action, a life full of virtue, faith that prevails, gentleness of heart, and strength of spirit. I am grateful for the evidence of your continued work in my husband's life. Thank you for leading him deeper into relationship with you, which affects his relationships with me and all others. Father, sometimes our culture looks on qualities like kindness and gentility as synonymous with weakness; impress upon _____'s heart that your kingdom is counter-cultural, and that these attributes show evidence of his choice to follow Christ. Impress him to allow his mind and demeanor to be influenced in these ways. Plant a desire in his heart to do good as often as he can. Give him courage to always let his light shine before others for your glory. Help him relax into the plans that you have for his life, and for the people that he draws toward you. I love his good-humored spirit and desire to develop friendships and relationships. I love the way his eyes gleam when we are surrounded by people! You gifted him with those characteristics, Lord. Keep him steady in the circle of your love, knowing that standing in your will affects his influence on all others. It is when we connect and identify with people that we can truly show them our authentic message of Jesus.

And you yourself must be an example to them by doing good works of every kind. (Titus 2:7a NLT)

In the same way, let your light shine before others, so that they may see your good works and give glory to your Father who is in Heaven. (Matthew 5:16 ESV)

Death and life are in the power of the tongue, and those who love it will eat its fruits. (Proverbs 18:21 ESV)

Reflection:
Do I remind my husband of the powerful influence he has on others? Do I encourage him to share his influence and life stories with others? Do I consider the influence that my words have on my husband and on others?

Notes

_____

_____

_____

_____

_____

_____

_____

_____

_____

_____

14.

Choices in Battle

$\mathscr{I}$ thank you for my husband and the warrior spirit that you have placed within him, Heavenly Father. Your word describes a spiritual warrior after God's heart as a man of authenticity and a man of integrity. I pray that my husband will be that kind of warrior in every circumstance. May he always wield that fighting spirit with a temperament of grace and love. Give him wisdom not to pursue battles from a selfish or jealous heart. Father, scripture tell us in Ephesians 4 that we will be angry at times, but instructs us to not sin in our anger or let the sun go down on our anger. I pray that you will give my husband purity of heart and strength to make these choices. May he look for and receive your guidance for when to fight valiantly and when to simply walk away. I pray that he spend his energy fighting for kingdom principles, rather than against flesh and blood. Mature his spirit with a compassion for others that governs as love and forgiveness. Instill within him your strategic battle plan and the confidence to be your soldier. Remind him that taking his faith into every battle will extinguish the arrows coming at him from the evil one. Fill him with knowledge about the armor of God and with a desire to intentionally put it on daily, even before the crisis comes, so that he will be prepared when evil comes his way in any form. I ask for your grace in giving _____ the ability and knowledge to apply securely the belt of truth around his waist, the breastplate of righteousness, and fit his feet with readiness of the gospel of peace; that he learns to shield himself with faith, to put on the helmet of salvation and carry the sword of the Spirit by carrying the word of God in his heart. Prepare his heart to pray through every situation with prayers of thanksgiving and requests, and to be alert throughout his life for anything that would separate him, or those he fights for, from you.

For you equipped me for strength for the battle; you made those who rise against me sink under me.
Psalm 18:39 ESV

Finally, be strong in the Lord and in His mighty power. Put on the full armor of God, so that you can take your stand against the devil's schemes. For our struggle is not against flesh and blood, but against the rulers, against the authorities, against the powers of this dark world and against the spiritual forces of evil in the heavenly realms. Therefore put on the full armor of God, so that when the day of evil comes, you may be able to stand your ground, and after you have done everything, to stand. Stand firm then,

with the belt of truth buckled around your waist,
with the breastplate of righteousness in place, and
with your feet fitted with the readiness that comes
from the gospel of peace. In addition to all this, take
up the shield of faith, with which you can extinguish
all the flaming arrows of the evil one. Take the
helmet of salvation and the sword of the Spirit,
which is the word of God. And pray in the Spirit on
all occasions with all kinds of prayers and requests.
With this in mind, be alert and always keep on
praying for all the Lord's people.

Ephesians 6:10-18 NIV

Reflection:

Am I undergirding my husband with truth? Am I helping
him to focus on Christ so that he can be prepared for the
conflicts of this world? Does my husband know that I'm in
his corner?

Notes

_____

_____

_____

_____

_____

_____

_____

_____

_____

_____

15.

Peace

Heavenly Father, I thank you for being the source of provision for every single thing that we need. Deepen in my husband every day the realization that he is yours, and that you will never leave him. Give him daily reminders that you are his shepherd, his guide, his best friend, his father, his almighty King. Impress upon his spirit that you care about him. Ebb away any feelings of unworthiness or insecurity that prevent him from feeling loved. Wash away any legalistic influence that may affect his judgments or actions. Gently breathe in his direction that you want him to know you, and that you long to spend time with him and keep him close. Help him to trust in you. Help him to walk with you. Train him to turn his strife and pressures into praise and prayers, and let Christ displace worry at the center of his life. Help his unbelief in difficult times. When he hurts, Father, or when he is confused, put in his heart a desire to walk in your will, so that he will experience the peace like a river that we're told about in Isaiah 48:18 (ESV). Give him a strong spirit so that his faith will prevail through all circumstances. I pray that you flood his soul with your peace regardless of the storm around him. Place in _____'s heart a sensitivity to the leading and prompting of the Holy Spirit, and a peace that comes from knowing that you will put him in the right place with the right people at the right time. Though it may be frightening for him to give up control, help him surrender fully to your will. Father, we know that your desires for us are greater than anything we could ask or imagine. Impress upon him that the weight of the world is not on his shoulders, because Jesus carried that weight to the cross. Give him the unparalleled peace that comes along with knowing that you, the Creator of the universe, care about his needs and his life. Help him to see that your peace, which passes all understanding, can be ever-present in his life, no matter what circumstances may come.

You keep him in perfect peace whose mind is stayed on you, because he trusts in you. (Isaiah 26:3 ESV)

Do not be anxious about anything, but in everything by prayer and supplication with thanksgiving let your requests be known to God. And the peace of God, which surpasses all understanding, will guard your hearts and your minds in Christ Jesus. (Philippians 4:6–7 ESV)

Helper. Rescuer. Defender.

*"I have said these things to you, that in me you may
have peace. In the world you will have tribulation.
But take heart; I have overcome the world."
(John 16:33 ESV)*

Reflection:
*Does my husband see me at peace? Does he see me in sync
with the Prince of Peace? Does he get to see my freedom
from disturbances of this world as a result of my choice to
remain focused on Jesus?*

Notes

_____

_____

_____

_____

_____

_____

_____

_____

_____

_____

_____

_____

_____

_____

_____

16.

Significance and Purpose

*H*elp him to know who he is and whose he is… the adopted and loved son of the one true God. Perfectly created by you for your purpose. Thank you for making my husband Your heir and coheirs with Christ. Thank you for promising him that because he fully accepts Jesus' sacrifice, that he no longer must maintain his identity in this world, but that he becomes pure, blameless, and forgiven. Thank you for loving him unconditionally. Thank you for the fact that my husband belongs to you, Jehovah Jireh, the provider of his needs. Remind him that you knew him before he was born, that you created him uniquely and for a unique purpose, and that you will never leave him. Place the imprint in his soul that he is made in your image, Father God, and that he is important enough for you to have sent your son to be crucified for his personal salvation. I ask that you overcome any lingering belief of wrongful judgments on him or toxic words that have been spoken over him; help him to grasp the truth that he is of great significance to you; that he is a son of the King and a citizen of the kingdom! Give him the strength to overcome hurtful words that have impaled his spirit and lean in, instead, to the truth of your Word. You've told us in Deuteronomy 32:10 that my husband is the apple of your eye, and in John 3:16 that your son died for him because he believes in Jesus. Help him know when he looks in the mirror that he is eternally loved and valuable to you; that absolutely nothing can separate him from your love. I pray that you lay these thoughts on his heart, especially in times when he is feeling weak or powerless or uncertain.

Even if my father and mother abandon me, the Lord will hold me close. (Psalm 27:10 NLT)

For I know the plans I have for you, declares the Lord, plans to prosper you and not to harm you, plans to give you a hope and a future. (Jeremiah 29:11 NIV)

No, in all these things we are more than conquerors through him who loved us. For I am convinced that neither death nor life, neither angels nor demons, neither the present nor the future, nor any powers, neither height nor depth, nor anything else in all creation, will be able to separate us from the love of God that is in Christ Jesus our Lord. (Romans 8:37-39 NIV)

Reflection:

Am I strong enough in who God says that I am to remind my husband of who he is, too? Does my husband get a glimpse of God's adoration for him in the way I see him?

Notes

17.

Commitment and Perseverance

*T*oday I pray for you to breathe spiritual strength, commitment, and perseverance into my husband's soul. Draw him to you with your kindness and mercy. Show him the long game, God, and give him strength to keep going when he is weary and stressed. Give him cleansing breath and an acute ability to focus on what is before him. Give him mental acuity and a spirit of restfulness in his soul. Pierce his soul with your purpose for his life. Guard him from spending energy chasing things that are not from you. Guide me to encourage him that your promises and his commitment to you trump emotions, complacency, and resistance. Allow him to see your face and know that Heaven is the game plan, and that all that he is dealing with on this side of Heaven is for his good and to your glory. Show him your inordinate ability to use every person and circumstance for good that he cannot yet see. Like in Psalm 23, although he may walk through valleys of darkness, give him the courage to keep his eyes on the eternal light of Jesus. Renew his mind to see Jesus as the perfect example of faith and perseverance. Help him to breathe out his inadequacies, and to breathe in your all-sufficiency. Encourage him to choose truth and commitment over convenience or feelings. Lead him forward into the perfection of his faith, Father, and let his mind be governed by only You. Strengthen his faith to persevere in the ways of Christ when the going gets rough, knowing that Christ came to overcome the things of this world. Teach him to guard his heart. Show him where feelings can be deceptive and help him continually develop an awareness for choosing actions based on faith, not feelings.

Above all else, guard your heart, for everything you do flows from it. (Proverbs 4:23 NIV)

Do not be conformed to this world, but be transformed by the renewal of your mind, that by testing you may discern what is the will of God, what is good and acceptable and perfect. (Romans 12:2 ESV)

As for us, we have all of these great witnesses who encircle us like clouds. So we must let go of every wound that has pierced us and the sin we so easily fall into. Then we will be able to run life's marathon race with passion and determination, for the path has been already marked out before us. We look away from the natural realm and we focus our attention and expectation onto Jesus who birthed faith within us and who leads us forward into faith's perfection. His example is this: Because his heart was focused on the joy of knowing that you would be his, he endured the agony of the cross and conquered its humiliation, and now sits exalted at the right hand of the throne of God! (Hebrews 12:1-2 TPT)

Reflection:
Am I encouraging with my husband in a way that helps him overcome the hiccups of life and keep moving toward his goal? Do I help him to remain focused on the long-term goal when the wind and waves come?

Notes

_____
_____
_____
_____
_____
_____
_____
_____
_____
_____
_____
_____
_____
_____
_____
_____

18.

Ability to Find Beauty

eavenly Father, I thank you for your gifts of beauty that are all around us. Over and over in your word, we read about the wonders of your creation and about how heaven and earth praise you, the seas and everything that moves in them. Allowing our attention to rest on your creation helps us to really see your majesty and behold your works. Help my husband to notice the beauty of your creation in everything... in the splendor of sun rises, in the horizon, in seascapes, in mountains, in me, in others, in animals, in the colors of the sunsets. May he learn to commune with you in nature and to praise you with his whole heart. Bring to his mind the gentle beauty of your love and gifts in people and in nature and even in the work you've given him to do. Encourage him to meditate on your lavish love, blessings, and kindness. Call to his mind your faithfulness to fulfill every promise you have made. Help him live in a place of gratitude for what we have, for all that you have blessed us with, realizing that all of it is of you and from you. Let him be mindful to always give you glory for the blessings in our lives. Thank you for equipping my husband with everything he needs to circumvent whatever the enemy throws in his path, so that we can thrive in the beauty that you intended for our lives. Develop in him the desire to steward it well with an attitude of gratitude. May he experience a sense of your splendor and power in your creation and consider it a personal gift of serenity, peace, and a calming influence. Thank you for my husband's boyish sense of wonder and curiosity about the skies and the stars and the ocean; allow that to gravitate him toward sensing the beauty of the Creator of the Universe in all things.

You are the Lord, you alone. You have made heaven, the heaven of heavens, with all their host, the earth and all that is on it, the seas and all that is in them; and you preserve all of them; and the host of heaven worships you. (Nehemiah 9:6 ESV)

When I look at your heavens, the work of your fingers, the moon and the stars, which you have set in place, what is man that you are mindful of him, and the son of man that you care for him? (Psalm 8:3–4 ESV)

On the glorious splendor of your majesty, and on your wondrous works, I will meditate. (Psalm 145:5 ESV)

Reflection:

Do I remember to rest my soul in your creation from time to time? Am I smitten with your creation and its beauty? Do I reflect the beauty of your creation for those around me?

Notes

19.

The Irrevocable Gift to Praise

*J*esus, your mercy and grace are boundless. May
_____ experience your loving kindness personally
for himself and know that Jesus has all authority over
all things in Heaven and on Earth. Give him eyes to
see your splendor and put a song of praise on his lips.
Praising you magnifies our vision of you as our almighty
God (Psalm 69:30 AMP) and gives us the opportunity
to sense the very presence of you, Lord. Psalm 22:3
teaches us that you inhabit the praise of your people;
you live there, and we can be especially close to you
through our praise. Praising you helps us to escape
negativity, return to humility, and remember that we
need you guiding our lives, Father God. Help him
learn to praise you both when the waters are smooth
and when his spirits need to be lifted. Demonstrate
the power of praise in my husband's life, Father, as
you've promised to reward those who earnestly seek

you (Hebrews 11:6). Give him insight that the enemy actually flees when he praises you! May he find the peace and contentment that you are sovereign and in powerful control of all things. I pray that you help my husband develop a supernatural faith and the true joy of praising you no matter the circumstances. May he connect with you through praise and prayer; may he know the comfort of your promise that you have overcome the world. Grant him strength to praise you even when solutions don't seem evident.

Pray without ceasing. (I Thessalonians 5:17 KJV)

Let everything that has breath praise the Lord! Praise the Lord! (Psalm 150:6 ESV)

I will praise the name of God with a song; I will magnify him with thanksgiving. (Psalm 69:30 ESV)

Reflection:
Does my husband see me praising God in good times and in bad? Do I set an example for praying and praising the name of Jesus?

Notes

20.

Meaningful Friendships

*F*ather, I praise you for giving _____ encouraging friendships that care about him. Thank you for providing godly people, and specifically godly men, to speak into his life and character. I thank you in advance for new relationships you will foster as mentors specifically for this season of his life. I pray that he will be open to those new relationships, and that he will find common interests with them. We know that iron sharpens iron and that you are using special relationships to pour into and sharpen my husband, as he pours into and sharpens them. May he know that by following you he will never walk alone, that he has in you a true friend that will stick closer than a brother (Proverbs 18:24 ESV). Give him insight to realize that the friendships and brotherhood he has with others is also a gift from you. I know that the company he keeps will either lift him up or drag him down. Give him discernment between the two. Protect him from being influenced by anyone who would sway him with negative influence. Draw him toward the right friendships, toward those people who will truly be reliable friends and hold each other accountable to the light of your word. Magnify for him those relationships with others who are followers of Jesus; lead him to walk with the wise. Remove anyone from his circle who would knock my husband off the path and into darkness. Prompt his spirit to recognize red flags and to keep risky relationships at bay, and to extend the effort to keep the right friendships in his inner circle. May he be a good friend and blessed with good friends throughout his lifetime.

Walk with the wise and become wise, for a companion of fools suffers harm.
(Proverbs 13:20 NIV)

Iron sharpens iron, and one person sharpens another.
(Proverbs 27:17 CSB)

Do not be misled: "Bad company corrupts good character." (1 Corinthians 15:33 NIV)

Reflection:

Am I a good friend to my husband? Does my circle of friendships show a group of people that lift me up, and that I also lift? Do I give energy into maintaining good friendships, or is it just too much work for me? Do I encourage my husband to spend some time with other men who pour godly character into his life?

Notes

_____

_____

_____

_____

_____

_____

_____

_____

_____

_____

_____

_____

_____

_____

_____

_____

_____

_____

_____

21.

Satisfaction and Contentment

*F*ather, sometimes our hearts are restless, and we get carried away in our culture of more, more, more. We are bombarded constantly with subliminal and overt messages about what else we "need". Help us to remember that life is about much more than grinding and hustle and possessions. Sometimes we think the grass is greener in another pasture, breeding discontent in our own; guard us against this. Guard us against selfish thinking and actions. I pray that you give us the grace to take captive every thought and make it obedient to Christ (2 Corinthians 10:5), and to focus on you. Keep us grounded in kingdom principles, and away from pretense. Keep my husband's heart pure and free from the dangers of comparison and coveting. Help us to strive for more only in the paths that you would have us follow. You have placed dreams within our hearts that have the potential to advance the kingdom and accomplish your purposes. All the blessings that we have are from you alone. Bring our hearts to a place where we are never afraid to give, and give generously. Help us to intentionally stay with you, our shepherd, rather than rashly chasing after things that are not for us to have. We have experienced times of plenty and times that are scarce, Lord, and you always provide. Turn our hearts so that we can learn to be content always, to rest in your love and provision. Teach us to look around and see our abundance in times when it is tempting to think we don't have enough.

But godliness with contentment is great gain, for we brought nothing into the world, and we cannot take anything out of the world. But if we have food and clothing, with these we will be content.
(1 Timothy 6:6–8 ESV)

Speaking to the people, Jesus continued, "Be alert and guard your heart from greed and from always wishing for what you don't have. For your life can never be measured by the amount of things you possess." (Luke 12:15 TPT)

Keep your life free from love of money, and be content with what you have, for he has said, "I will never leave you nor forsake you."
(Hebrews 13:5 ESV)

Reflection:

*Can my husband see contentment and joy in my life?
Have I considered my influence on him with regard to
wanting more? Do I display gratitude for our home and
the things that we have?*

Notes

22.

To Seek You First

$\mathcal{W}$e praise you, Lord. We thank you for your greatness, for your sovereignty, for your abundant love. We thank you for your provision in our lives. You've promised in your word that if we seek the kingdom first, that all these things will be added to us. Help us to trust and believe in your word. Place within my husband (and myself) the desire to develop the discipline of seeking you first. Teach _____ to study your Word in a way that develops maximum understanding. I praise you for the times that my husband prioritizes you. I pray that you give him favor when he makes difficult and counter-cultural decisions that put you first. Let it be more than a habit, Lord; let it become our life-giving routine to seek first the kingdom daily. Allow him to sense my respect for him as he demonstrates this kind of humility and reverence for your leading in his life. Let us come to know what your kingdom really looks like and how to bring it to this earth. In Matthew 7:7 (ESV) you tell us to "Ask, and it will be given to you; seek, and you will find; knock, and it will be opened to you." Give us the grace to just come to you, first and always. I ask that you increase our capacity to trust you for provision. You are a good, good father; you have promised us that you hear our prayers. I bring to you a reminder, Lord, of your promise in Lamentations 3:25 (ESV), that "the Lord is good to those who wait on him, to those who seek him." My husband and I are seeking you, Lord; we are waiting on you.

But seek first the kingdom of God and his righteousness, and all these things will be added unto you. (Matthew 6:33 ESV)

And my God will supply every need of yours according to his riches in glory in Christ Jesus. (Philippians 4:19 ESV)

Seek the Lord and his strength; seek his presence continually! (1 Chronicles 16:11 ESV)

Reflection:

Does my husband see me seeking God in my daily routine? Could I encourage this practice by providing a way for us to seek the Lord together in our daily life?

Notes

_____

_____

_____

_____

_____

_____

_____

_____

_____

_____

_____

_____

_____

_____

_____

_____

_____

_____

_____

23.

Anxiety, Hopelessness, and Depression

*H*oly Father, you are worthy of praise, even when we are wreaked with worries and concerns. Sometimes we need a gentle reminder to lay them at the throne. Give me the grace to perceive the times when _____ is wrestling with anxiety, hopelessness, or depression, even though he may hide it well. Help me treat him with extra grace and tenderness in those times. When my husband is wrought with troubles and stress, keep him in the center of your will. Remind him to seek your face and to cast every concern at the feet of Jesus. Remind him that very few things are permanent on this side of Heaven, and that his moment of despair will pass when your light drives away the darkness. Even in the darkness, Lord, remind him that you are right there with him and that you always provide a way through. Remind him that you are his advocate (1 John 2:1), the almighty, the Alpha and Omega (Revelation 1:8), his counselor, everlasting father, and the Prince of Peace (Isaiah 9:6). In these moments, help him to remember that he is a beloved son to you, and that you are his deliverer (Romans 11:26). Comfort him, console him, and carry him through, when he is challenged and when the storms of life come. Fill him with peace, Lord. And no matter what he faces, Father, give him one more bit of strength to grasp the hope that you offer, for your word tells us in Isaiah 40:31 NIV "But those who hope in the Lord will renew their strength. They will soar on wings like eagles; they will run and not grow weary, they will walk and not be faint."

Fear not, for I am with you; be not dismayed, for I am your God; I will strengthen you, I will help you, I will uphold you with my righteous right hand. (Isaiah 41:10 ESV)

Trust in the Lord with all your heart, and do not lean on your own understanding. In all your ways, acknowledge him, and he will make straight your paths. (Proverbs 3:5-6 ESV)

Even though I walk through the valley of the shadow of death, I will fear no evil, for you are with me; your rod and your staff, they comfort me. (Psalm 23:4 ESV)

Reflection:
Do I remember the hope of the Lord in troubled times? Do I encourage my husband and others in this way?

Notes

_____

_____

_____

_____

_____

_____

_____

_____

_____

_____

_____

_____

_____

_____

_____

_____

_____

_____

_____

_____

24.

Spiritual Leadership and Fatherhood

*F*ather, I come to you in awe of the good father that you are for us. I am so thankful for your love. Thank you for bringing my husband out of darkness and into your marvelous light! I pray over my husband today that he will not hesitate to take any place of spiritual leadership that you have for him. Thank you for the opportunities to serve, for serving others gives him the opportunity to reflect your glory and character. Guide his heart and mind to look to your example of parenting and not necessarily to his earthly experience. He is in a position of leadership for many, both as a father and as a father-figure. I can't imagine the burdens he carries at times, nor the weight that he feels. Create an awareness within him as people look to him for guidance. Fill his heart with compassion and gentleness. I ask that you remind him of his purpose and that your strength is always available for him to operate within; remind him that your strength and love is all that he needs. Help him see himself through your loving eyes; ignite a desire in him to expand into new territories of leadership that you have for him. Thank you for ever-increasing blessings and favor on him as you guide him to positively impact others or to serve those in need. I ask that you guide him in seeking the qualities of a godly man, and that you would gift him with the energy and desire to continue to grow. Create within him a desire to partner spiritually with me so that, together, we can spread your love and advance your kingdom.

But you are a chosen race, a royal priesthood, a holy nation, a people for his own possession, that you may proclaim the excellencies of him who called you out of darkness into his marvelous light.
(1 Peter 2:9 ESV)

Pay careful attention to yourselves and to all the flock, in which the Holy Spirit has made you overseers, to care for the church of God, which he obtained with his own blood. (Acts 20:28 ESV)

Be free from pride – filled opinions, for they will only harm your cherished unity. Don't allow self-promotion to fide in your hearts, but in authentic humility put others first and view others as more important than yourselves. Abandon every display of selfishness. Possess a greater concern for what matters to others instead of your own interests.
(Philippians 2:3–4 TPT)

Reflection:

Does my husband see me worshiping our holy God as a Father? Does my husband know that I see him as a good father?

Notes

25.

Humility

*H*eavenly Father, your word advises us that humility comes before honor (Proverbs 18:12 KJV). Lord, humility is often misunderstood in our world today, and false humility creates deceit and a danger zone for our hearts. Humility is not meekness or weakness, nor is it devaluing who we are in your divine creation; rather it is a heart posture of complete dependence on you as our Lord and Savior. Father, create a humble heart in my husband that conveys in his daily life. I ask that self-sufficiency and pride never be his guiding force. God, we know from James 4:6 that you "oppose the proud but show favor to the humble." Help him to walk humbly with others and not in arrogance or with a lofty mindset. Help him to value others according to the unique way that you made them and not comparatively. Grant him the wisdom that humility is not thinking less of himself but thinking of himself less. Give him mindfulness of your provision and an attitude of gratitude that contributes to humility. I pray that you develop within him a clarity of who he is… a loved and valued son of the one true King… with a humility that postures his heart toward you in every circumstance of every day. I ask that you bless his life with a fulfillment of what is required by you in Micah 6:8 (NLT), "to do what is right, to love mercy, and to walk humbly with your God."

The fear of the Lord is the instruction of wisdom, and before honor is humility. (Proverbs 15:33 NKJV)

Laying your life down in tender surrender before the Lord will bring life, prosperity, and honor as your reward. (Proverbs 22:4 TPT)

Humble yourselves before the Lord, and he will exalt you. (James 4:10 ESV)

Reflection:

Have I spent time with God truly learning what humility is? Do I convey humility in my own life? Do I encourage my husband to see himself not in weakness, but in humility?

Notes

_____

_____

_____

_____

_____

_____

_____

_____

_____

_____

_____

_____

_____

_____

_____

_____

_____

_____

_____

26.

Kindness and Forgiveness

Father God, I praise you for your loving kindness and forgiveness toward us. Thank you for redeeming us with such a loving act as sending your only son to the cross to pay the price for our sins. I pray that you will impress deeply upon me and my husband to respond in kindness and be quick to forgive; ourselves, each other, and others. Sometimes we need forgiveness, Father, and sometimes we need to forgive, but it is impossible for us to have relationships among imperfect people without forgiveness. Posture our hearts in humility to realize when we need forgiveness and when we need to extend it. Grow our spirits toward managing our hurts and grievances with an eternal perspective. Help us to reflect your grace in the way we live, speak and act. Give us abounding energy within our relationships to look for creative ways to show kindness and to identify with others. Father, we know that kindness is a part of the fruit of the spirit, and one of the ways that we know we are walking with the Holy Spirit and maturing as believers. Soften our hearts, Lord, to intentionally develop kindness and forgiveness. Help us to remember that these virtues start at home, and from that foundation, spread into the world. Fill my husband's heart with the grace to forgive others as he has been shown grace by the blood of Christ. May you be glorified in the kindness and forgiveness that we show to each other and to those around us. I pray that you are glorified in the way we handle our marriage, and our relationships with others.

And be kind to one another, tenderhearted, forgiving one another, even as God in Christ forgave you. (Ephesians 4:32 NKJV)

"And whenever you stand praying, forgive, if you have anything against anyone, so that your Father also who is in heaven may forgive you your trespasses." (Mark 11:25 ESV)

Do not repay evil for evil or reviling for reviling, but on the contrary, bless, for to this you were called, that you may obtain a blessing. (1 Peter 3:9 ESV)

Reflection:
*Am I developing my kindness and forgiveness muscles
with intention? Would my husband describe me as being
kind and forgiving with him?*

Notes

27.

Marriage Focused on God

𝒥come to you grateful for the blessing of my husband and for our marriage. Through the craziness of life in this world, Lord, help us to rely completely on you. Lord, we invite you to be the foundational rock of our marriage. _____ and I decided at the beginning for this to be a union of three, and we want to keep you at the center of our marriage. The bond between us is infinitely stronger with you at the center, just like a cord of three strands is not easily broken (Ecclesiastes 4:12). We are called to love and honor you first. Give us the blessing of a marriage where we both choose respect and honor. Give us grace to overcome annoyances, frustrations, misunderstandings, and arguments. I pray that we can remind each other never to allow anything to become idolized within our marriage over you, Lord, including outside influences, careers, generational patterns, past problems, parents, in-laws, children, possessions, or ourselves. Father, you know that we are both broken, and brought plenty of hurts with us to this relationship. I pray that you prompt us to seek healing in our hearts when those wounds arise. May we always look to you first, Lord, and may we always be better individuals because you have brought us together. Strengthen our marriage, Lord, and help us to foster your ideas for each other with grace and love. Grant us vision for our marriage and the desire to speak life into each other. Give us grace to base our marriage on faith and not just sight; to be more focused on commitment than feelings. Help us to lift each other with our words and with our silence. Grant us the ability to walk in step and to live harmoniously. Above all, help us to love each other deeply with the kind of love fashioned after your unconditional love for us. I pray that you always get the most and the best of my husband and me, and from the union of our marriage. Thank you for the times where you've provided for us when we couldn't see a way through the situation, for nothing is impossible with you (Luke 1:37).

> *"Haven't you read the scriptures?" Jesus replied. "They record that from the beginning 'God made them male and female.'" And he said "'This explains why a man leaves his father and mother and is joined to his wife, and the two are united into one.' Since they are no longer two but one, let no man split apart what God has joined together." (Matthew 19:4-6 NLT)*

> *Beloved, let us love one another, for love is from God, and whoever loves has been born of God and*

*knows God. Anyone who does not love does not
know God, because God is love. (1 John 4:7-8 ESV)*

*Love never gives up, never loses faith, is always
hopeful, and endures through every circumstance.
(1 Corinthians 13:7 NLT)*

Reflection:
*Is my life a reminder for us to keep God in the center of
our marriage? Do I keep myself in check and not idolize
anything above our marriage covenant? Do I gently
remind my husband to do the same?*

Notes

_____

_____

_____

_____

_____

_____

_____

_____

_____

_____

_____

_____

_____

_____

_____

28.

Purity of Heart and a Teachable Spirit

eavenly Father, I lift my husband's heart to you today. I love how my husband is always learning new things, and specifically ask that you would make him hungry for spiritual growth. Lord, 1 Corinthians 10:31 teaches us to do everything we do with the single purpose of accomplishing your will and purpose. This is what a pure heart does. I earnestly ask that _____ will seek only you with his whole heart and commit everything that he does to your glory. Protect him from those with opinions who would cause him to stray from your will and your way. Purify his heart and renew his spirit. Grow him past any deceit, malice, ill will, prejudice, or hatred. Teach him to leave behind any rapid anger and conclusions of his youth, and to search for biblical truth. Help him to look for the good in others, and to always try to see the message and not the messenger, your beings and not their shortcomings.

Help him realize that you know every portion of his heart, his thoughts, his plans; help him learn to take every thought captive and obedient to Christ. Grow _____ in wisdom as he investigates the scriptures and spends time with wise friends and counsel. Create in him a desire to study scripture and a passion to learn your ways. Teach him that your word is truly living, and that you will continue to grow his knowledge, faith, and wisdom as he continues to search for your ways.

*"Blessed are the pure in heart, for they will see God."
(Matthew 5:8 NIV)*

*Create in me a clean heart, O God, and renew a
right spirit within me. (Psalm 51:10 ESV)*

*Run as fast as you can from all the ambitions
and lusts of youth; and chase after all that is pure.
Whatever builds up your faith and deepens your love
must become your holy pursuit. And live in peace
with all those who worship our Lord Jesus with pure
hearts. Stay away from all the foolish arguments of
the immature, for these disputes will only generate
more conflict. (2 Timothy 2:22-23 TPT)*

*"And Solomon, my son, learn to know the God of
your ancestors intimately. Worship and serve him
with your whole heart and a willing mind. For the
Lord sees every heart and knows every plan and
thought. If you seek him, you will find him. But if
you forsake him, he will reject you forever."
(1 Chronicles 28:9 NLT)*

Reflection:

When my husband looks at me, does he see the single purpose of bringing glory to God in everything I do? Does he see me coming to the fountain at the throne of grace to renew my spirit?

Notes

_____

_____

_____

_____

_____

_____

_____

_____

_____

_____

_____

_____

_____

_____

_____

_____

_____

_____

_____

_____

29.

Your Will for His Life

$\mathcal{F}$ather, our world is so fast paced that we often forget to consult you as we rush into actions or reactions, then want you to approve. It doesn't lead to your best for our lives. Lord, I praise you for having a good and perfect will for each of us. I praise you for the comfort of Jeremiah 29:11 that assures of your specific plans to prosper my husband, and to give him hope and a future. I pray Your will for my husband's life; not his own, not mine, not ours. I pray that he will realize that any obsession with self-reliance and his own plans apart from you is a dead end and instead learn to trust your actions in his life. Thank you for the fact that we only need to ask you to guard our hearts and minds against straying from your will. In every circumstance of life, I pray that we look to you and honor your will for our lives. Lord, help us to focus on you. We want to live in obedience to your word;

we know that your will has reason and purpose. Draw close to us and grow us in wisdom so that we can hear your voice and instruction. I ask that my husband and I learn to walk with you so that we can discern your will for our lives together. Your ways are better than our ways and your plans are more magnificent than ours, greater than anything we could ask or imagine! We ask that you reveal your will for our lives in ways that we can perceive and understand. I thank you that you invite us to continually develop relationship with you and honor you as our creator, our savior, our father, our king. Lord, give us humble hearts to listen and obey.

Your word is a lamp to guide my feet and a light for my path.(Psalm 119:105 NLT)

He has shown you, O man, what is good; and what does the Lord require of you but to do justly, to love mercy, and to walk humbly with your God? (Micah 6:8 NKJV)

Many are the plans in a person's heart, but it is the Lord's purpose that prevails. (Proverbs 19:21 NIV)

Reflection:

Does my husband have the benefit of watching me seek God's will for my life decisions, both big and small? Do I encourage him toward listening and obedience to God, regardless of what I think is the best idea?

Notes

_____

_____

_____

_____

_____

_____

_____

_____

_____

_____

_____

_____

_____

_____

_____

_____

_____

_____

_____

30.

Grace to Serve

Heavenly Father, we can get so caught up in our own lives and in serving our own interests. Help my husband to become fully aware that your intent for us on this earth is to serve; to serve you, Lord. To serve our families and our communities for the purpose of advancing the kingdom. Grow us, mature our hearts away from selfishness and self-serving. Lead us away from thinking that everything revolves around ourselves and our own family, but rather anyone that you would have us impact in some way. Give us grace to think outside ourselves and commit to serving you with all our hearts and with all our souls. Give my husband eyes to see needs and opportunities to serve in ways that will glorify you. Give us the grace to see the needs, and then act on them. Help us not to fall within the trap of craving center stage for ourselves, but to do everything to your glory. Give us courage not to shy away from serving because we're hung up on our inadequacies or fears, Lord, but to know instead that you will equip us to any task that you ask of us. Help us rely on you to create divinely crossing paths with people who need our help, people whose help we need, and people we can team up with to serve more efficiently. Thank you for giving us ways to serve, and for changing our hearts to want to make a difference. Bless our marriage with joy as we learn to serve together. In all ways, let us honor you through our lives and through our marriage.

"For even the son of man came not to be served but to serve, and to give his life as a ransom for many." (Mark 10:45 ESV)

"Give, and it will be given to you. Good measure, pressed down, shaken together, running over, will be put into your lap. For with the measure you use it will be measured back to you." (Luke 6:38 ESV)

Only be very careful to observe the commandment and the law that Moses the servant of the Lord commanded you, to love the Lord your God, and to walk in all his ways and to keep his commandments and to cling to him and to serve him with all your heart and with all your soul. (Joshua 22:5 ESV)

Reflection:

Do I look for opportunities to serve rather than to judge? Am I an encourager to my husband in ways that he can serve God and others? Do our lives bring glory to the King of kings?

Notes

_____

_____

_____

_____

_____

_____

_____

_____

_____

_____

_____

_____

_____

_____

_____

_____

_____

_____

_____

_____

31.

Cadences I Don't Recognize

As much as I know my husband, Father, I trust that you know him more intimately as his Creator. As much as I love him, God, I know that you loved him first and more. I fully submit my husband to you and your authority. You have the authority, Lord, to use whatever means of communication you see fit to impact his life. You know when there is a chasm between us in our perceptions or understanding of each other. You know the depths of his heart and the longings of his soul and the rumblings in his spirit. Sometimes, there are responses or reactions that I do not understand; sometimes, my spirit cannot put into words the feeling that I know something is amiss or that my husband needs help. When I do not know what to do or say, Father, I remind you that you have promised to translate the groanings of my spirit and do what you know needs to be done according to your infinite and perfect will. I praise you for loving us so much that you would be my ezer in those moments. Help me know that I do not have to always know or understand; I only need to trust my God and redeemer. I praise you for giving me the grace to release my husband fully to you and to your will.

For I am the Lord your God who takes hold of your right hand and says to you, Do not fear; I will help you. (Isaiah 41:13 NIV)

Likewise the Spirit helps us in our weakness. For we do not know what to pray for as we ought, but the Spirit himself intercedes for us with groanings too deep for words. (Romans 8:26 ESV)

"For my thoughts are not your thoughts, neither are your ways my ways," declares the LORD. "As the heavens are higher than the earth, so are my ways higher than your ways and my thoughts than your thoughts. (Isaiah 55:8-9 NIV)

Reflection:

Do I put my full trust in God for the things that I do not know or understand? Do I spend time in worry and fret instead of casting every care at the feet of Jesus?

Notes

_____

_____

_____

_____

_____

_____

_____

_____

_____

_____

_____

_____

_____

_____

_____

_____

_____

_____

_____

One Final Prayer

*H*eavenly Father, you are an awesome God and a good, good father. Thank you, God, for giving _____ to me. He is a blessing in my life. He is extraordinary, for you created him in your own image and in an extraordinary and wonderful way. Because of your perfect love, I can love him, experiencing some of Heaven's grace and glory on this side of the divide. Thank you for that. I praise you for changing my life in that way. I thank you for the bonds and the family that our union has created. I thank you for uniquely creating us and for having planned desires and purpose for our lives. I praise you for the love and newness of life that you have given us by bringing us together, and for the plans that you have for our shared life. Thank you for never being too busy to hear the prayers of a wife who loves her husband; in fact, thank you for the blessing of assigning me with sovereign authority to be his helper. Thank you for the immense blessing of watching you work supernaturally in his life and to see the changes that result. Thank you for caring about our lives. Thank you for caring about our dreams. Thank you for caring about the longevity and impact of our marriage. Thank you for being for us. Grant me the wisdom to model Christ in my life to my husband, loving him with the grace and beauty with which you have shown me love.

See what great love the Father has lavished on us, that we should be called children of God! And that is what we are! The reason the world does not know us is that it did not know him. Dear friends, now we are children of God, and what we will be has not yet been made known. But we know that when Christ appears, we shall be like him, for we shall see him as he is. All who have this hope in him purify themselves, just as he is pure. (1 John 3:1-3 NIV)

We love each other because he loved us first. (1 John 4:19 NLT)

Love is large and incredibly patient. Love is gentle and consistently kind to all. It refuses to be jealous when blessing comes to someone else. Love does not brag about one's achievements nor inflate its own importance. Love does not traffic in shame and disrespect, nor selfishly seek its own honor. Love is not easily irritated or quick to take offense. Love joyfully celebrates honesty and finds no delight in what is wrong. Love is a safe place of shelter, for it never stops believing the best for others. Love never takes failure as defeat, for it never gives up. Love never stops loving. (1 Corinthians 13:4-8a TPT)

Connect with Kim

I have written these words in obedience to God as my husband was away from our home for ten months working. It is amazing how God uses time and circumstances, especially difficult ones, to call us deeper into His will. Know that if you are reading this book, that I have prayed for your life and that it will somehow change for the better. I pray that your new awareness and habits result in a stronger marriage, changing circumstances for your husband and/or yourself, or simply changed hearts that are a little more in step with our Creator. God is always good and will go to extraordinary lengths to put these words in front of those who need to hear them, those who need to establish new prayer patterns, and those who need a friend. I would love to hear from you!Feel free to email me and let me know how your life changes as you begin to truly submerge your husband and marriage in the love of Jesus Christ. You are loved!

book.kimgordon@gmail.com

Acknowledgments

Thank you to my Heavenly Father for whispering to me to write my prayers and for breathing on the results in every way.

From the depths of my heart, thank you to my Stewart. Your support and understanding through this process has been amazing. I'm so grateful that you're in my corner and so blessed to be your wife.

Sometimes, God gives the gift of a friend who brings the grace of Heaven to this earth. He has given me such a friend, and she's been mine for decades. We have done life together; every part of it. I owe humble gratitude to you, Steph Stewart, for doing life with me. Thank you for translating and understanding my eastern Kentucky dialect, and for fixin' it when necessary! Thank you for copy editing this work a million times. Thank you for being my friend, unwaveringly. I thank God for you literally every day.

My kind and loving God also chose to bless me with an amazing individual who has become a mentor and, indeed, a mother to me. My sweet Momma Jane, thank you for being true to God's calling on your life so that I would have the deep desire to pattern my life after yours. Thank you for showing me what it looks like to truly be like Jesus. Thank you for supporting every crazy idea that I have and everything that I do. Thank you for helping me learn to pray more intensively and to praise bigger. I thank God for you and your wisdom every single day.

Thank you to my late earthly father for always encouraging me to write. I know you'd be thrilled about this, Dad. I miss you so much; there is such a hole in my life here without you.

Special thanks to Debra Grady for 'finding' and praying over my work. Thank you for your kindness and patience with me as a rookie, for your availability to me, and for helping me learn this process. Thank you for your dedication to putting what God is doing right now into print.

Kim Gordon is available for author interviews.
For more information contact:

Kim Gordon
Advantage Books
info@advbooks.com

To purchase additional copies of this book or any
other book that we publish, visit our bookstore at
www.advbookstore.com

Orlando, Florida, USA
"we bring dreams to life"™
www.advbookstore.com

www.ingramcontent.com/pod-product-compliance
Lightning Source LLC
Chambersburg PA
CBHW071755090426
42737CB00012B/1827